Auntie Anne
MY STORY

by Anne Beiler
illustrated by Freiman Stoltzfus

Auntie Anne's, Inc. Publications

Auntie Anne, My Story

Written by Anne Beiler
Illustrations by Freiman F. Stoltzfus

Book design by Freiman F. Stoltzfus
© Copyright 2002 by Auntie Anne's, Incorporated

FIRST EDITION

Library of Congress Control Number: 2002093165

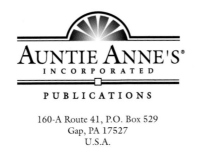

AUNTIE ANNE'S®
INCORPORATED
PUBLICATIONS

160-A Route 41, P.O. Box 529
Gap, PA 17527
U.S.A.

ISBN 0-9722638-0-2

Summary: In *Auntie Anne, My Story,* Anne tells the story of her life in her simple, straightforward way, and beautiful illustrations capture scenes along her journey. This storybook biography is perfect for folks young and old, whose lives will be touched by Auntie Anne's simple philosophies.

Color separation and layout by Lancaster Ultra-Graphics

Printed by Acorn Press, Lancaster, Pennsylvania, USA, 1-800-356-3264

My story begins on January 16, 1949, when I was born on this farm surrounded by the rolling hills of Lancaster County, Pennsylvania. I was the third of eight children. My parents were members of the Amish community, a people of German heritage who have lived here since the middle of the eighteenth century. We spoke a dialect called Pennsylvania German. At that time, we had no electricity and our only transportation was a horse-drawn buggy.

My mother and father were simple, hardworking people. My mother, Amanda, taught me many valuable lessons. She instilled in me a desire to strive for excellence in all my endeavors, telling me, "Do it with will, do it with might; things done by halves are never done right."

My mother is well known for her beautiful handwork, and for many years she had a quilt shop, selling to visitors from all over the world. Years later, she made quilts for Presidents Ronald Reagan and George Bush. I was so proud to accompany her to the White House to personally present a quilt to President Reagan.

My father, Eli, was a very generous man. He donated land from our farm so that a church could be built there. Eli and Amanda went to the Bowery Mission in New York City many times to help serve meals to the homeless men. On a number of occasions, they brought these men back to our farm. One was named Carl, and he lived in our home for a time, helping my father with his work and sharing meals at our table.

As a very young child, I was taught the value of hard work. My family spent many hours gardening, cleaning, baking, sewing, mowing, and washing. We found happiness and meaning in labor, and I never considered it a punishment to be awakened at 6:00 a.m. on a cold morning to help Dad milk the cows or gather eggs for my mother. Mom also taught me and my sisters to sew and make our own dresses.

In the spring we planted and watered our fields and gardens. In summer, we picked strawberries, cherries, and peaches, tomatoes, peas, and corn. We canned fruits and vegetables in preparation for the long winter months.

When the sun was setting and all the evening chores had been completed, the family gathered together around a long table laden with the foods of the season. We sat side by side on the hard wooden benches, and my father led us in a simple prayer:

> God is great, and God is good,
> And we thank Him for our food.
> By His hands we are all fed;
> Give us Lord, our daily bread.
> Amen.

We did not have a television or radio, so we learned to entertain ourselves and one another. My mother often read Bible stories to us in the evening, and then we would sing together. Our family could not afford to take many vacations. On special summer afternoons, Mom would pack a picnic lunch for us, and we would walk to the covered bridge not far from our home. We took turns sharing the one bike we owned, or we splashed and waded in the cool waters of the creek.

There was also a pond not far away, and often at the end of a hot day, we could swim as a reward for all the work done that day.

I attended the Linville Hill Amish Mennonite School in Paradise, Pennsylvania. I loved to study and learn, but I really enjoyed recess, when I could play outdoors. I remember this jump rope verse:

> Down in the meadow
>   where the green grass grows
> There sat Anna
>   as sweet as a rose
> She sang,
>   she sang so sweet
> Along came Jonas
>   and kissed her on the cheek
> How many kisses did he give her?
>   One, two, three....

I always loved my mother's kitchen. I was a very young girl when she began to patiently teach me to gather and combine delicious ingredients for the many specialties contained in her recipe box. By the time I was 12, I was working alone, baking pies and cakes for a market stand in Philadelphia where my parents and I worked on weekends. How I loved to go to the big city! I was so curious about the world outside my little community, and I was fascinated by the many people of different nationalities, languages, and colors.

On Sunday mornings, I awoke early as always to help with the daily chores. But, aside from the necessary milking of the cows twice a day, there was to be no Sunday work. By 8:30 a.m., everyone was washed and dressed, and ready to pile into our big black car for the drive to church. The church was a large red brick building with white trim and plain clear windows. There were always many friends there, as well as uncles, aunts, and cousins. The women and girls sat on the left side of the church, and the men and boys on the right, all in neat rows. A basket was passed to all the rows, and my father always put in a small offering from the money he made the week before. We sang songs in German and English, without instruments to accompany us. After returning home, there was a great big lunch for all. Many times, my parents would invite a family to our home for Sunday dinner, and we would have as many as 20 or more people at our table. After the meal, the afternoon was spent quietly, in rest and reflection.

Christmas was always magical! My family exchanged gifts, and we shared a wonderful noontime feast. One of the best things about the holiday was the Christmas program at school. All the children participated, singing songs and reciting poetry. I often had a special part, a song to sing, or a role in the pageant. At the end of the evening, we all held a candle and sang:

Stille Nacht, heilige Nacht!
Alles schläft, einsam wacht
Nur das traute, hochheilige Paar.
Holder Knabe im lockigen Haar,
Schlaf in himmlischer Ruh.
Schlaf in himmlischer Ruh.

(Silent night, holy night
All is calm, all is bright
'Round yon virgin, mother and child
Holy infant, so tender and mild
Sleep in heavenly peace
Sleep in heavenly peace.)

In winter, the nights were long and cold. We waited impatiently for the snow and ice, and for the pond to freeze over. Then we would bundle ourselves in warm coats, gloves, and brightly colored knit scarves, and trudge across the fields carrying our skates. Many of my friends and neighbors were there, and we spent many carefree hours gliding on the ice that was as smooth as glass, playing "Fox and Geese", "Crack the Whip", and "Prisoner's Base." At midnight, we all returned home for toast and hot chocolate before falling into bed, happily exhausted.

At night, Mom tucked me and my sisters, Becky and Fi, into our big squeaky bed. We snuggled under the cozy quilts, giggling and whispering. Together we said a bedtime prayer:

> Müde bin ich, geh' zur Ruh
> Shliesse meine Augen zu;
> Vater, lass die Engelein
> Uber meinem Bette sein.
>
> (I am tired, I go to rest,
> I tightly close my eyes,
> Father, let your angels kind
> Watch over my bed tonight.)

We loved to sing together! All our bedroom doors would be open at night, and often we would sing our family to sleep. Years later, we began to sing publicly, and we made four recordings of our blended voices. We were called the Triple Hearts Trio.

At the age of 14, I took my first job as a waitress at a nearby truck stop. There I learned that you must put people before profits. I soon learned that serving others kindly put tips in my apron pocket! Other waitresses often complained about how rude this truck driver was, or how ugly that one was. Being the only Amish Mennonite waitress there, I stuck out like a sore thumb because I didn't look or act the same. Serving and giving were part of my upbringing, and I always tried to remember that kindness and a smile will open the door into anyone's heart. That never fails.

One night at a friend's birthday party I was introduced to a tall young man named Jonas Beiler. He was 18, and had a spark of humor in his eyes and a humble strength about him. I sipped my root beer and tried to act natural, but my friends noticed how he and I kept exchanging glances. "Jonas is so handsome," they teased. "We heard he likes you!"

That evening, someone said, "How about a game of 'Walk a Mile'?" It's a favorite among older Amish Mennonite youths, where couples hold hands and walk down the lane, changing partners as they walk. When my turn came to walk with Jonas, I found myself blushing and my heart beat faster.

Soon Jonas and I started courting. From our first date, we were so comfortable together, like we'd known each other forever. He had grown up Old Order Amish, the most conservative of the Amish-Mennonite groups, but he'd chosen not to formally join the church when he came of age at 16. Instead of buying a horse and buggy, Jonas pursued his fascination with cars. He bought old junkers, took them apart and rebuilt them, figuring out how they were put together as he went along. By the time we met, he had his own auto repair shop. "I don't know if I can explain it," Jonas said, "but I was drawn to this life. It felt right for me, fixing things people depend on."

That's how I felt about Jonas. He felt right for me. In September of 1968, we were married.

In time, we had three beautiful daughters: LaWonna, Angela, and LaVale. A tragic accident claimed the life of little Angela when she was only 19 months old. Jonas and I were devastated, and it took many years for us to recover from our terrible loss. Our marriage was shaken, but we were determined to save our family. Together, we worked through our grief and the difficulties that we faced. Jonas and I talked for many hours, untangling and reconciling our feelings about Angie, and the aftermath of her death.

Just as he became consumed with repairing old cars, it was during this time that Jonas became very interested in how he could help people put their lives back together, just like ours had been mended. A dream was born! He began to work toward opening a counseling center, where people of our background could find help and healing.

In 1977, Jonas, the girls, and I moved to Texas, along with my two sisters and their families. A few years before, we had all left the conservative Amish Mennonite church - not to reject our parents or their faith, but because we sought greater spiritual freedom. We were asked to help develop a church in Jacksonville, Texas, and we lived there for 10 years. I truly loved my time in the big state of Texas. It was so different from Pennsylvania, and full of wonderful, generous Southern people, many who remain close friends today. I learned a lot about myself, and about life and people while living there. I was exposed to a much bigger world, and it had a profound impact on my life.

In 1987, we decided to move back to Pennsylvania. I really didn't know what I was going to do when I returned home. But, within a few weeks, I was asked to manage a soft pretzel store at a farmer's market, and I decided to take the job.

Seven months after I began working at the farmers' market, I heard of a booth that was for sale at a market in Downingtown, PA. We borrowed money from Jonas' dad and bought it - sight unseen. I sold pizza, stromboli, ice cream and hot, hand-rolled soft pretzels, which have always been a favorite of Lancaster County's Dutch population. The pretzels were certainly the most popular item, and I began to notice their appeal to people of all ages.

For two months, I tinkered with the recipe, but I continued to find the results disappointing. "I'm ready to give up on the pretzels," I told Jonas. "They look bad and taste terrible."

"Since when do we give up so easily?" he teased. "I'm going to the store to buy ingredients that I used to use when I helped my mother bake in her kitchen." I said to Jonas, "If you think your idea will work, then go buy the ingredients, add them to the pretzel mix, and we'll see." That's exactly what Jonas did, and guess what? The "new" recipe produced a *great* pretzel - "better than the best" we had ever tasted! The Auntie Anne's pretzel was born! Almost immediately, lines began to form in front of our store, and we could hardly make the pretzels fast enough.

Before long, our customers didn't seem to be interested in anything else *but* our pretzels. I began to make batches of fresh lemonade, which I thought would be a perfect accompaniment to the taste of hot, salty pretzels.

"Something this good deserves its own special name!" Jonas declared.

In February of 1988, we christened the little pretzel stand Auntie Anne's Hand Rolled Soft Pretzels, after the name my 30 nieces and nephews affectionately call me. I chose my favorite shade of blue for my store's signs and countertops.

In less than a year, we opened a second stand, then a third and fourth. In the beginning, I tried to do it all - I bought and delivered products, and I helped the stores any way I could. Our garage soon became a cluttered office and warehouse as we began to grow. Soon, I asked my family and friends to help me mix batches of pretzels, paint signs, construct booths, deliver ingredients to the stores, and work at the market stands.

I'm often asked about the distinctive shape of the pretzel. When we needed to design the pretzel shape for the business, my sister Becky made a photocopy of one of my pretzels from the oven, and that became the pretzel shape you see at our stores today.

News of the pretzel phenomenon began to spread, and before long I received my first request for a franchise. I have to admit that I knew nothing about franchising. I look back now and often laugh at the many mistakes I made while learning by trial and error. But I've been so fortunate to have capable people by my side, and together we've accomplished much. Now we help qualified people from around the world to open their own stores in shopping areas, train stations, and airports. Imagine my surprise when I discovered pretzel lovers all over the United States, not to mention in places as far away as Japan, Thailand, Malaysia, Saudi Arabia, the Philippines, and England!

Over the years we've added many new flavors and products, but our original recipe remains the same. Today, Auntie Anne's is still a family-centered business where each customer feels like a welcome guest - a place where people can go and say, "That's the way it used to be." Remember the days when people treated you with respect and kindness? That's what I want in every store.

Today my life is quite different than what I dreamed it would be as a child. I am a businesswoman, but first and foremost, I am a wife, mother, and grandmother. The time I spend with my daughters and grandchildren brings me my greatest joy. Life for me has not always been easy, but I'm truly grateful for all that God has given to me, for the wonderful gifts of friends and family.

I still love to visit Auntie Anne's stores, and every year Jonas and I get on our motorcycles and travel for a few weeks across America, dropping by to see our friends. I'm as surprised as you might be to find myself driving a Harley-Davidson® motorcycle, breezing down the highway with my husband right behind. It sure is a long way from the horses and buggies we grew up with, but my mother never lets me forget who I am, and where it all began. I still live just a few miles from the old farmhouse where I was born, and I still go to work every day.

In 1992, Jonas opened the doors to the Family Resource and Counseling Center, fulfilling his dream of offering free counseling to the Amish and Mennonite community, which is funded by profits from our pretzels. I was taught to always give back a portion of the gifts God gives me, and to share my blessings with those in need. It is my passion!

In the end, I've found that the lessons my mother taught me years ago remain true today: honor God and family, be kind, give generously, and do unto others as you would have them do to you. Those lessons have guided me well in both my business and my family life, and I pray that they may guide you as well!